Winning Gold

Also by Lorna Schultz Nicholson

In the Recordbooks series
Fighting for Gold: The Story of Canada's Sledge Hockey Paralympic Gold
Pink Power: The First Women's World Hockey Champions

In the Lorimer Sports Stories series
Against the Boards
Cross-Check!
Delaying the Game
Holding
Interference
Northern Star
Roughing
Too Many Men

Winning Gold

Lorna Schultz Nicholson

James Lorimer & Company, Ltd., Publishers
Toronto

James Lorimer & Company Ltd. acknowledges the support of the Ontario Arts Council. We acknowledge the support of the Government of Canada through the Book Publishing Industry Development Program (BPIDP) for our publishing activities. We acknowledge the support of the Canada Council for the Arts for our publishing program. We acknowledge the assistance of the OMDC Book Fund, and initiative of Ontario Media Development Corporation.

Cover design: Meredith Bangay

Library and Archives Canada Cataloguing in Publication

Schultz Nicholson, Lorna
    Winning gold : Canada's incredible 2002 Olympic victory in women's hockey / Lorna Schultz Nicholson.

Includes index.
ISBN 978-1-55277-472-4 (pbk.).—ISBN 978-1-55277-473-1 (bound)

    1. Women hockey players—Canada—Juvenile literature. 2. Winter Olympic Games (19th : 2002 : Salt Lake City, Utah)—Juvenile literature. 3. Hockey—Canada—History—21st century—Juvenile literature. I. Title.

GV848.6.W65S385 2009   j796.962'66   C2009-906863-X

James Lorimer & Company Ltd., Publishers
317 Adelaide Street West,
Suite #1002
Toronto, ON
M5V 1P9
www.lorimer.ca

Distributed in the U.S. by:
Orca Book Publishers
P.O. Box 468
Custer, WA USA
98240-0468

Printed and bound in Canada.

Manufactured by Webcom in Toronto, Ontario, Canada in November 2009.
Job # 364662

To the women of the 2002 Olympic Hockey Team, for believing! Canada is proud of you.

Contents

Prologue

The January day was dark, damp, and overcast. Cassie Campbell and Vicky Sunohara walked in the misty rain along the Vancouver seawall with Bob Nicholson, President of Hockey Canada. He had flown in to meet with the captains to discuss what was wrong with the Canadian Women's National Hockey Team. *Why had they lost seven games in a row to the USA?* he wanted to know.

Maybe the team needs some changes, thought Bob.

At the 1998 Olympic Games in Nagano, Japan, Canada had lost in the gold-medal game to the USA. Everyone had expected the women to win. The loss had been a huge upset for the team, Hockey Canada, and Canadian fans. Now, four years later, no one wanted another silver medal. Gold was expected in the 2002 Winter Olympics in Salt Lake City.

Cassie and Vicky told Bob that the pre-Olympic losing streak was the players' fault, and not the fault of the coaches. Earlier in the day, Bob had met with the assistant captain of the team, Hayley Wickenheiser. He had met with her separately to get true reactions. She had told him the exact same thing.

The players needed to pull it together. Team Canada had a lot of experienced players. But for some reason, they were struggling. The breaks just never seemed to come their way. They needed a win.

The team was in Vancouver because they had one last game to play against the USA. The eighth pre-Olympic game would be held at the state-of-the-art General Motors Place the next day. After seven losses, Bob had concerns about the team. He tried to stay positive: If they won in Vancouver, they would head into the Olympic Games with at least one win. *That would certainly help*, he thought.

After the walk, Bob decided to stay to watch Game 8 in the pre-Olympic set. He would also be going to the Olympic Games, which began the next month in Salt Lake City, Utah, USA. There, he knew, Canadians would accept nothing less than their women's team bringing home the gold medal.

1 Final Faceoff

On Tuesday, January 8, 2002, Danièle Sauvageau addressed her team in the dressing room at General Motors Place in Vancouver. The media had called the game they were about to play the "Final Faceoff." The coach of the Canadian Women's Olympic Team didn't have a lot to say. She'd had her players practise the power play over and over again. She'd made them train hard. Sometimes the workouts she gave them were as hard as the workouts she'd had to do herself to become an RCMP officer. She'd even taken them to an army base that summer. There, she had them do some of the same drills the Canadian army had to do, running obstacle courses and climbing over cement walls.

Coach Danièle told them their lines. She talked about a few strategies they'd been working on in practice. The power play was important. And so was the penalty kill. The US team was known for their power play.

Over six thousand fans had come to watch the women play. Many were dressed in Team Canada jerseys and waved the Maple Leaf. They were very vocal. The players knew the game was being nationally televised. People from all across Canada would be hoping for a win.

Cameras snapped as the players stepped onto the ice.

With total confidence, Kim St. Pierre, starting goalie for that night's game, took her place in net. She shuffled back and forth in the crease. Today she had been given the green light to be goaltender for Canada. But both Kim and goalie Sami Jo Small wanted to earn the coveted spot of starting goaltender. The decision as to who would be the starting goalie for the Olympic tournament had not yet been decided.

When the whistle blew, the players lined up at centre ice. With the drop of the puck, the fast pace began. The Canadians started off strong and were out-shooting the USA. But then Canadian forward Lori Dupuis took a charging penalty. The clock read 3:48. The USA was on the power play.

The USA gained possession and immediately cycled the puck in the Canadian zone. Kim followed each play, moving from side to side in her net.

Shot after shot, Kim made saves. The Canadians managed to clear the puck out of their zone a couple of times, but the USA came right back in.

Then a shot came from the blue line. It was a hard one. The puck flew straight to the back of the net. The red light went on. Goal for the USA.

For the rest of the period, Coach Danièle kept a close eye on Kim from the bench. Kim had made two unbelievable saves in that first period. One was a booming shot from the point. The other was a glove-hand save on a shot that came from the slot. But was she playing well enough to be the starting goalie in Salt Lake City?

At the end of the first period, the Canadians were still down 1–0, even though they had outshot the USA 7–3.

The Canadians came back on the ice in the second period fired up. They were

Colleen Sostorics looking for a pass in pre-Olympic play.

only down one goal. At 12:43 in the second period, the Canadians' hopes soared. Forward Caroline Ouellette picked up the puck and passed it to Cassie. Cassie passed it to Hayley. Hayley fired the puck, sinking it to the back of the net. The crowd roared. The Canadians were on the scoreboard!

The score was still 1−1 when the buzzer announced the end of the second period. The Canadians had outshot the USA in the second period and were leading shots on goal by 21−11.

Just 1:18 into the third period, forward Jennifer Botterill rushed in to forecheck the USA defense. She managed to steal the puck behind the American net. With a quick wrist shot, she bounced the puck off the American goaltender and into the net. When the red light flashed, the team went crazy. Jennifer's unassisted goal had given the Canadians the lead for the first time in the game. Now they just had to hang on to it.

The Canadians continued to battle. They shot and shot at the USA goalie but she made save after save.

Then at 13:13 the USA somehow slipped one past Kim.

Everyone looked at the clock. The score was tied at 2–2. At the bench, the Canadians told each other they could still win. So far they'd outplayed the USA. All they had to do was keep shooting and put another one in the net. They lined up at the faceoff. The puck dropped. They battled.

Just over one minute later, the USA blasted a shot towards Kim. When it hit the back of the net, the Canadian players were stunned.

The Canadian women all looked up at the clock: 14:31. They had over five minutes to score and tie the game.

Although they worked hard and outshot the USA, the goal they needed never happened. When the buzzer went to end the game, the Canadian team had lost their eighth straight game to the USA by a score of 3–2. But they had outplayed their opponents. How could they have lost again? This was not the record they wanted heading into the Olympic Games.

Eight-and-Uh-oh!

Game 1 Oct. 20, 2001, in Salt Lake City:
USA 4, Can 1

Game 2 Oct. 23, 2001, in San Jose:
USA 4, Can 1

Game 3 Nov. 27, 2001, in Ottawa:
USA 5, Can 2

Game 4 Nov. 28, 2001, in Montreal:
USA 4, Can 3

Game 5 Nov. 30, 2001, in Hamilton:
USA 1, Can 0

Game 6 Jan. 5, 2002, in Chicago:
USA 3, Can 1

Game 7 Jan. 6, 2002, in Detroit:
USA 7, Can 3

Game 8 Jan. 8, 2002, in Vancouver:
USA 3, Can 2

2 Talking it Through

The Canadian women silently filed into the dressing room after the game. One by one they sat on the bench and leaned back against the concrete wall. No one attempted to undress and get out of their sweat-soaked equipment. The door leading to the lobby remained locked. They needed time to absorb what had happened, and they didn't want anyone in the room, not even the coaches.

After five minutes, some of the players

broke the silence with comments about the game, saying that if they kept trying, they would get better. But Hayley was still stinging from the loss and she just couldn't listen. She didn't want to fluff this over. So instead, she raised her voice to talk openly about her frustration. Upon hearing how upset Hayley was, many of the players became emotional.

As captain, Cassie realized she needed to control what was going on. "Hayley has brought up some good points," she said. "We need to talk this through."

Cassie's words were like a dam breaking. They gave the players the okay to vent. Some yelled, some whispered, others just talked. Many cried.

For more than forty-five minutes, they remained in the dressing room, in their equipment, discussing what had gone wrong. They hashed over their losses. They talked through the problems, and they

Team Captains

There were three team captains on the women's hockey team. The captain was Cassie Campbell, who is the most captained player in the history of hockey in Canada. Assistant Captain Vicky Sunohara played in the first ever Women's World Hockey Championships in 1990 in Ottawa, Ontario. That was the year the Canadian Women's Hockey Team wore pink and white jerseys! Assistant Captain Hayley Wickenheiser was playing in her third Olympic Games in 2002. Hayley had played hockey in the 1998 Winter Olympics and she had also played on the Canadian Softball Team in the 2000 Summer Olympics.

talked about what they needed to do to get better.

Then the team decided that they still believed they could win at the Olympics. They would have to put the eight losses behind them. Gold was still within reach.

The time they spent in the dressing

*Cassie Campbell was the captain of the 2002
Women's Olympic Hockey Team.*

room that night was the turning point for
the Canadian Women's Olympic Hockey
Team. They decided then and there how

much they wanted to win gold. Some of the women had played on the 1998 Olympic team. They knew what it felt like to come home with silver.

When they had finished, Cassie said, "What a story this will be."

While the players were inside the dressing room, André Brin, Manager of Media Relations for Hockey Canada, had reporters line up outside. Many of the reporters were on deadlines and had to get their stories to press.

Coach Danièle had also stayed outside the dressing room. The players needed to work this out for themselves. She had already told them they had practice the next day back in Calgary — a morning practice. She wasn't going to give them any rest. Last she had heard she was still coach, so she eased the anxieties of the deadline-driven reporters pacing in the hallway by answering questions.

"Right now we have all the big pieces, and I'm going to search for the little thing [to make a difference]," Danièle said. "We're going to compete. Battle to the end. You can't push a button and say, 'Fifth floor, please.' In order to get to the top you've got to climb the stairs one by one."

When the players finally started filing out of the dressing room, there was a calm surrounding them.

Jennifer stopped to talk to a reporter from the *Vancouver Sun*. "It's easy to understand how from the outside you can look at the record and be very concerned. However, within the team we still feel extremely confident in knowing we're going to come together and peak at the right time with our performance at the Olympics."

Goaltender Sami Jo Small was next on the *Sun* reporter's hit list. From the bench, she'd had a front-row seat for the game. "It does matter that we've lost . . . don't get me wrong," she said. "But there is really only one game that really matters and that's February 21 [the Olympic gold-medal final]."

Across the country many doubted that the Canadian Women's Hockey Team could win an Olympic gold medal. Eight losses were just too much to come back from. Under a headline that read, "Canadian Women confident of managing miracle on ice," a *Calgary Herald* sports reporter wrote: "The losses have been piling up like dirty laundry in the bottom of a closet. They're up to eight stinkin' defeats and counting now."

But the players had decided that night that they could still win. They still believed. Would that be enough?

3 Tough Choices

The team arrived back in Calgary after midnight. They were staying in dorms across the street from the Father David Bauer arena in Calgary, where they trained.

The next morning, a number of players showed up to practice a few minutes late. When they got there, the door was locked. Coach Danièle had locked it. Any player who wasn't there at the exact time she told them to be there, wouldn't be practising with the team.

Only eight players out of twenty-one ended up practising that morning.

While some of the players were standing outside, Hockey Canada personnel were inside their offices at the arena discussing the team.

Bob Nicholson's phone had rung all night with calls from the media, and was still ringing that morning. The media's questions were rapid and cutting: What was wrong with the women's program? What did he think about the eight losses in a row? What plans did he have for the team now? Was he going to make any changes?

The team had played well. They had lost, but they had definitely stepped up their game. He had decided he wasn't going to make any changes to the coaching staff.

Bob wasn't the only one thinking about changes. For weeks, Danièle had been in discussions with her three assistant coaches, Wally Kozak, Melody Davidson, and Karen Hughes. They talked constantly about what they could do to make the team better and get them on the winning path. They had gone through each player and discussed her role on the team.

After a long talk, the coaches were ready to make some roster changes.

They met with veteran forward Nancy Drolet in private and told her she was cut from the team. Cherie Piper would be taking Nancy's spot.

Hockey Canada sent out a press release January 14. It read: "Canada's National Women's Team Adjusts Roster for Salt Lake City."

The press release had the media buzzing. The *Calgary Herald* wanted to write about this shake-up. They talked to Danièle. She said, "I was hired to put the best team on the ice, and this is what we thought was the best decision, and we

The 2002 Canadian Women's Hockey Team and the Hockey Canada management team at the Father David Bauer arena prior to leaving for Salt Lake City.

made it. It was very well thought out and not something we decided overnight. It has been going on for weeks and months."

Some of the players didn't take the announcement well. Many felt insecure about their position on the team. If Nancy could be let go, then who was next? And many on the team were going to miss Nancy. She had been a national team

The Nancy Drolet Appeal

On January 17, 2002, Nancy Drolet registered an appeal to get back on the team so she could play in the Salt Lake City Olympics. Nancy's appeal made national headlines and became a heated issue. On January 27, 2002, she lost her appeal.

member and a veteran player and was well liked.

At the next practice after the announcement, Cherie Piper arrived ready to take her new place on the team.

Cherie had been working hard, moving up the hockey ladder. She'd been disappointed to have been left off the Olympic roster in November, but had continued training hard with the team. She knew this was her big chance.

On February 6, the final members of the Women's Olympic Team boarded the plane for Salt Lake City.

4 Quote du Jour

Arriving in Salt Lake City, the team was taken to the Olympic Village to get settled in their rooms. After they unpacked their bags, they were told to meet so they could all get their accreditation. They lined up and got their photos taken, then the photos were put on a piece of paper and laminated. It was almost like getting a passport. And they had to wear this around their necks at all times. If they didn't, they wouldn't get into the Olympic Village, where athletes from all over the world, from every sport, were housed for their duration at the Olympics.

The Olympic Flame burns brightly during the Opening Ceremonies.

Once every player had their accreditation slung around their necks, it was
time to get ready for practice. In five days
they would step on the ice to play their
opening game in the 2002 Winter
Olympics.

Canada had been put in a round-robin
pool with Kazakhstan, Russia, and Sweden.
Their first game was against Kazakhstan.
The other round-robin pool was made up
of teams from Finland, China, Germany,
and Canada's powerful rival — the USA.
The winner from one pool would play the
second-place winner from the other pool
in the semi-final games. Then the winners
of the semi-finals would play each other
for the gold-medal game. The winner took
gold; the loser, silver.

The two teams that lost in the semi-
finals would battle each other in the
bronze-medal game.

The Olympic Games started with a

spectacular Opening Ceremonies. Wearing red leather Roots coats, striped scarves, and tam-style hats, the Canadian Women's team lined up at the athletes' entrance with the rest of the Canadian Olympians.

Rumours about security for that night had filtered through the Olympic Village. Just five months before, on September 11, 2001, the World Trade Center in New York City had been attacked by terrorists. Because of 9/11, the Americans had extra security in place. There were snipers on rooftops. Helicopters flew overhead.

At the entrance, the Canadians listened to the President of the United States, George W. Bush, speak. They heard the Mormon Tabernacle Choir sing. Then the crowd hushed as a flag from the World Trade Center was raised. It was an emotional moment for everyone. A beautiful display of fireworks then began as the athletes entered. Speed skater Catriona

Le May Doan carried the Canadian flag. The Canadian group included 157 members, the fourth-largest at the Games.

The team's spirit was good following the Opening Ceremonies. For two days the Canadian Women's Hockey Team practised and did dry-land workouts. Getting out of Canada and into the Village had given them time to concentrate.

As a team, they decided that for motivation they would put together groups to come up with a *quote du jour* for each game. The quotes were meant to inspire their teammates to play the best they could. The team had to keep believing that they could win the gold. In the first group were Jennifer, forward Tammy Lee Shewchuk, forward Kelly Béchard, and Sami Jo.

The day of the game, the players stood before the rest of the team in the dressing room and said in unison, "Today's game

Team Roster

Goaltenders: Charline Labonté #32, Sami Jo Small #1, Kim St. Pierre #33

Defense: Thérèse Brisson #6, Isabelle Chartrand #73, Geraldine Heaney #91, Becky Kellar #4, Cheryl Pounder #11, Colleen Sostorics # 5

Forwards: Dana Antal #23, Kelly Béchard #24, Jennifer Botterill #17, Cassie Campbell #77, Lori Dupuis #12, Danielle Goyette #15, Jayna Hefford #16, Caroline Ouellette #13, Cherie Piper #7, Tammy Lee Shewchuk #25, Vicky Sunohara #61, Hayley Wickenheiser #22

will set the tone for the rest of the tournament. Only we can determine the message we send — let's make it one of no regrets."

After the quote, the players proudly slipped their jerseys over their heads. On the front of each jersey was Canada's heritage patch. This was the same patch that had been on the jerseys that the men's

team had worn in the 1952 Olympics, the
last time Canada had won gold in hockey
at the Games. The women were the first

*Vicky Sunohara wearing the Canadian heritage
jersey. Notice the Maple Leaf on the front.*

Canadian team in fifty years to wear the patch.

Coach Danièle had been waffling over who should go in net. Picking the starting goalie for the Olympics would be difficult. Goaltenders Kim and Sami Jo had been together for years on the National Team. Charline Labonté was the third goalie, but she wouldn't dress unless Sami Jo or Kim got injured. Whichever goalie was chosen for a game understood she was the lucky one. Sometimes that decision wasn't made until the last moment.

Kim had even been questioned by reporters about the issue. She had told them, "This is our fourth year together and we're used to it. Every year it's the same story and we're not really disturbed by who will be number 1 and who will be number 2."

Fortunately for her, Kim was named the starting goalie for the game.

Coach Danièle took her place on the bench. The kind of game they had to play today would be difficult. Kazakhstan was no match for her team. But Canada would have to play their best anyway. Games where one team was definitely better than the other team were hard because they could create bad habits like sloppy passes and lazy skating. They had to stay sharp.

5 Opening Game

When the whistle shrilled to start the game, the Canadians lined up at centre ice. The puck dropped, and bounced. And it seemed to keep bouncing. Passes missed sticks and the Canadian players seemed unsettled. At 2:30 in the first period, Kazakhstan took a holding penalty. Canada was to go on the power play.

Coach Danièle put out her first power-play line. They had practised and practised the power play. It took only three seconds for Hayley to rifle off a hard shot that sunk to the back of the net. The Canadians were on the scoreboard.

Although the play started at centre ice, it didn't take long to move back in the Kazakhstan end. The Canadians controlled the play and kept shooting on the goalie, but none of their shots made the red light go on. The Kazakhstan goalie was sharp and kept plucking the puck out of mid-air.

Then at 8:45, forward Cherie Piper smacked the rebound off a shot by linemate Dana Antal into the back of the net. Goal! The players hugged.

Less than one minute later, at 9:20, Canada was back on the power play. They passed the puck around but had trouble finding the net. The clock ticked down. Coach Danièle frowned. This wasn't the power play they'd practised. Then, with just eleven seconds left on the power play, defense Colleen Sostorics passed the puck

Tammy Lee Shewchuk breaking past a Kazakhstan player in the women's first Olympic Game.

to Cherie, who was hovering around in the slot. Cherie connected and fired the puck, but the Kazakhstan goalie dished out a rebound. Forward Vicky Sunohara swooped in for the rebound and scored Canada's third goal.

At the end of the first period, the score was 3–0 Canada.

The Canadian players talked about what they could do better. They were up 3–0, but they hadn't played great hockey. Their passes had been terrible.

Three minutes into the second period, Kazakhstan took another penalty and Canada was again on the power play. This time the puck moved from Colleen to forward Danielle Goyette to her linemate Tammy Lee Shewchuk, who scored her first goal of the game.

When Canada went into yet another power play, just five minutes before the end of the second period, forward Hayley Wickenheiser found the puck on her stick by fighting hard. She zipped towards the net. Firing the puck, she scored her second goal of the night. The assist went to Danielle.

Goalie Goods

• Kim St. Pierre is from Quebec. In 2001, at the World Championships, she was named top goaltender. Kim also played on the Quebec provincial softball team as a shortstop.

• Sami Jo Small made the 1998 Olympic team as third goalie. She didn't see any ice time. Sami Jo was also a really good discus and javelin thrower.

• Charline Labonté was the youngest player on the roster and had just made her debut on the National Team in 2001. Her first game was a shutout.

So far, Canada had scored four of their five goals on the power play. This pleased Coach Danièle, who had made them work on the power play over and over.

One more power-play goal was scored in the third period by Danielle on a pass from Hayley. The last goal of the game was scored by Vicky on yet another rebound from a shot by forward Jayna Hefford.

The shots were 66–11. When Kim took off her mask, she barely had sweat rolling down her face. Meanwhile the Kazakhstan goalie was exhausted. She'd made fifty-nine saves!

Even with a 7–0 victory, the Canadian team was not happy.

Defense Thérèse Brisson told a *Toronto Star* reporter, "It was shinny hockey, and we pretty much played that way. That was not great for us. In the first period, we were pretty much terrible."

Jennifer was a little more positive. "The USA is in the back of our minds, but we need to focus on each opponent."

Up in western Canada, a *Calgary Sun* reporter wrote, "Building toward the final against Team USA, Canada didn't exactly look like a well-oiled machine."

Another paper titled their article, "Seven Goals Not Enough."

The Canadian women had won one game and that meant they were one step closer to winning Olympic gold.

But the coaching staff and the players knew for this to come true they had a lot of work ahead of them.

6 Canada vs. Russia

The Canadian women had a day off between games to practise and regroup. During their down time, they gathered in the Olympic Village athletes' lounge to watch the other sports on television. There was huge controversy, too. In pairs figure skating, the Canadian team of Jamie Salé and David Pelletier had just lost the gold medal to the Russian pair. It was the talk of the Women's Hockey Team. They had all watched the event on television and were outraged by the judges' decision. And their team was playing the Russian hockey team next.

The Canadian Women's Hockey Team promised their skating friends a little payback. Vicky even said to a *Toronto Star* reporter, "We'll get them back for Jamie and David."

Cassie wrote up a note for her team and called it Captain's Corner. "*The definition of courage in the Defining Dictionary of the Living Russian language is 'Quiet Bravery, presence of mind in trouble or danger.'*" As a follow-up, in her own words, she wrote, "*How appropriate. Let's show the Russians our definition of courage and win it for David and Jamie!*"

As the team boarded the bus, ready to head to the arena, the players understood that they had to treat each game as important. They were a better team than Russia and would probably win. But in a tournament like the Olympics, a team had to get better every game. The tournament would only get tougher and tougher.

Before the game, Cherie, Caroline, Dana, and Kim got up and said their *quote du jour:* "So many people believe in you. Make sure you're one of them."

But when the puck dropped, the Canadians once again looked a little unsettled. The coaches thought the team looked as if they were playing down to the level of their opponents. The Russians were playing stubborn hockey and not giving Canada chances to score.

Halfway through the first period, the game remained scoreless. Finally, at 11:37, Hayley picked up the puck off the faceoff, powered to the net, and scored! The referee recorded it as an unassisted goal. Canada was on the scoreboard.

It was almost seven minutes later when Hayley passed the puck down along the boards. Danielle freed it and peppered a shot from the slot. Canada went to the dressing room with a 2–0 lead.

Just thirty-one seconds into the second period, Caroline took a pass from defense Geraldine Heaney and sent the puck over to Dana. Dana ripped off a quick shot to give Canada a 3–0 lead. Nine minutes later, Caroline, who was at the side of the net with the puck, looked up. She saw Cherie positioned perfectly in the slot. She passed the puck over, and Cherie one-timed it. The goal gave Canada a 4–0 lead.

A deflected goal started off the scoring seven minutes into the third period. Vicky sent off a high shot and Jennifer, hanging around the front of the net, deflected it past the Russian goalie. It was Canada's first power-play goal of the game.

Canada scored twice more before the end of the period. Their sixth goal was deflected two times before defense Isabelle

Caroline Ouellette ready to take a shot in Canada's game against Russia.

Chartrand — who was playing in her first Olympics — sunk it into the back of the net.

Fast Forwards Facts

• Dana Antal was born in Saskatchewan. In the 1997–98 season, Dana played in the National Swiss League.

• Kelly Béchard is from Sedley, Saskatchewan. Kelly won the Saskatchewan Provincial Badminton Championships in girls' doubles while in high school.

• Caroline Ouellette graduated from the National Police Academy in Quebec in the fall of 2000.

• Tammy Lee Shewchuk is a Harvard graduate. On January 7, 2001, she became the NCAA all-time leading scorer for women's hockey by scoring her 258th goal.

The final goal — number seven — saw Danielle weaving her way through the crowd and zinging a shot from the slot.

The score was 7–0 for Canada. Canada had outshot the Russians 60–6.

Sami Jo had been in net for Canada. The coaches were still trying to figure out who their starting goalie would be for the semi-finals and finals. Sami Jo had only had to stop six shots. The action she had seen was in the last twenty seconds when the Russians had put the pressure on. For those twenty seconds, Sami Jo had worked hard to keep her shutout.

After the game, Sami Jo met with a reporter from the *Winnipeg Free Press*. Winnipeg was her hometown. She said, "As a goaltender, yeah, it's one shot every ten minutes; but I don't really see it that way. It's an Olympic game, and I get to watch these girls score some goals and make some pretty plays. I mean, you never get bored out there."

Although the win was sweet, the Canadians couldn't rest. They had to stay motivated and keep up their intensity.

The *Toronto Star* summed it up by saying, "As impressive as 14 goals in two shutout games may sound, the Canadians still don't look sharp."

The women knew, too, that they had to step it up if they wanted to beat the Finns and the Americans.

7 Poetry in Motion

The energy in the Olympic Village made the women eager to play again. One more game would put them closer to playing in the gold-medal game. In the Village, they met athletes from different sports, and some of their National Hockey League heroes. The Canadian Men's Team was full of NHL stars. Also staying at the Olympic Village was men's team captain Mario Lemieux. The general manager of their team was hockey legend Wayne Gretzky.

It came as a huge shock to everyone when the Canadian Men's Team lost to Sweden 5–2 in their first game. This had not gone over very well with the Canadian media. The women talked about how their next game was against Sweden. They wanted to win. They wanted revenge for the men's loss. This would be the women's last game of their round-robin pool.

The *quote du jour* grouping for that game was a line that played hard together: Vicky, Lori, and Jayna. When they met to come up with a quote, they started laughing about all the fun they'd had over the year. Their talk reflected back on the entire season. It started in May when the team had gotten together to train. Vicky decided that their memories needed to be put into a poem.

When they finished, they printed it for everyone to read.

Before the game, Vicky, Lori, and Jayna recited the poem out loud. The entire team cheered when they came to the last two verses:

> *The challenge is ahead of us*
> *To beat the Swedes and Finns*
> *To play consistent hockey*
> *And do 20 second spins*
>
> *The moral of the story*
> *Is easy to define*
> *We've worked too hard this year*
> *To end up 0 and 9.*

Then the three women also shared a quote that they had found by French poet Paul Valery: "The best way to make your dreams come true is to wake up."

In no time at all the ice was ready. The Canadians filed out of their dressing room for the start of the third and final game of their round robin.

The period started off slow and Canada

went ten minutes without a goal. Finally, at 10:26, Jennifer took a pass from Tammy at Sweden's blue line and managed to stickhandle her way around a Swedish player on right wing. With a clear path to the net, she cut across the front of the crease and shoved the puck in on the far side of the net. The Swedish goalie didn't know what hit her. She didn't even have time to shuffle across to cover her net.

Although the Canadians hammered off nineteen shots in the first period, Jennifer's was the only goal.

Cherie opened up the scoring just four minutes into the second period by batting at a bouncing puck. Then Jennifer scored her second goal by deflecting a long shot from Geraldine at the point on a power play. Then it was Hayley's turn to score on a pass from Cassie. Hayley moved in close and shot the puck waist high. The last goal of the period was scored by Cassie as she steered the puck into the net on a pass from Danielle, who was behind the net.

The Canadians decided to turn up the heat.

In the third period, they were relentless. They had opened the scoring gates. They put in six goals from six different players. Goals were scored by Caroline, Jayna, Lori, Vicky, Dana, and Isabelle. All in all, ten players scored and the Canadians ended up beating the Swedes 11–0. Jennifer was the only one to score more than one goal. Jayna recorded four points with one goal and three assists, and Jennifer picked up three points. She added one assist to her two goals.

In net, Kim stopped all twenty-two shots that came her way. The shots on net were 70–22 for Canada.

In the *Winnipeg Free Press*, the headline read, "Different story as Women Play. This Canada–Sweden hockey game was all about Canada." The *Toronto Star* wrote, "Revenge: How Swede it is," and the *Calgary Sun* wrote, "Ladies get Swede Revenge."

Meanwhile, the Canadian women knew that, while it was nice that they had beaten the Swedes in such a one-sided game to get revenge for the men's team, they had a tough semi-final ahead of them.

Canada had finished first in their round-robin pool with a 3–0 record. But so had the USA. As expected, they had also won all three of their round-robin games.

The stage was set. Canada was to play Finland in the semi-final match up. The USA would meet up with Sweden for their semi-final.

But Finland would be no pushover. At the IIHF 2001 World Championships, they had taken a very young team. For this Olympics, they had brought back a lot of veteran players.

Vicky summed it up when she talked to the *Globe and Mail*, "I really think they [the Finns] came here with the idea that they can upset us or the USA."

8 Finns Fight to the Finish

A win in the semi-final game would take the Canadian Women's Hockey Team to the gold-medal final. A loss would take them to the bronze-medal game. They had to win. They had to have one more chance to play the USA.

Cheryl Pounder, Colleen, Becky Kellar, and Isabelle were in charge of the *quote du jour*. All of them played defense. The quote they came up with for the game was by American civil rights activist Martin

Luther King Jr.: "The ultimate measure of a person is not where they stand in moments of comfort and convenience, but where they stand in times of challenge and adversity."

From the first puck drop, it was clear to the Canadians that Finland had come to play and win. But really, that was no surprise to the Canadian team.

Just four minutes and two seconds into the game, Canada was given a power play opportunity. They shot and shot but the Finnish goalie stood-on-her-head and made save after save.

With just four seconds left on the clock in the power play, Thérèse blasted a slapshot from the point. The puck sunk to the back of the net.

At the 8:10 mark, Hayley picked up the puck and, on a breakaway, nipped it between the pads of the Finnish goalie.

For the rest of the period it looked as if

Canada would go to the dressing room with a 2–0 lead. Was this going to be another shutout game for the Canadians? Kim was in net and hadn't seen a lot of shots.

The clock read 19:35. The period would end in just twenty-five seconds. But then one of the Finnish players picked up the puck and made a spectacular move. Kim tried to make the save, but the puck settled in the back of the net.

The buzzer sounded, and the Canadians headed to the dressing room with a 2–1 lead.

The mood between periods was positive and calm. The Canadians were still up. They could easily beat the Finns.

They headed out for the second period sure of a success.

But something wasn't quite clicking for the Canadians. They were making some defensive errors and giving the puck away.

At 2:56, just short of three minutes into the period, the Finns popped the puck by Kim.

Not even one minute later, the Finns scored again. The Canadian players looked at each other. How had this happened? Somehow, the Canadians had let the Finns score two unanswered goals to take the lead.

In the stands, the Canadian fans were on the edge of their seats. Would this be another final faceoff game?

At that moment, the Canadians decided to put the pressure on. They peppered the Finnish goalie with shot after shot. But shot after shot, she made the saves. Her acrobatic moves stunned the crowd. Were the Finns going to pull the biggest upset in the history of women's hockey? Were they going to beat Canada to advance to the gold-medal game?

No other goals were scored in the

second period. The buzzer went and the Canadians went to their dressing room down by a goal.

The crowd murmured in the stands.

Between periods, the media barraged Hockey Canada President Bob Nicholson.

"What's happening to women's hockey?"

"Why are they losing?"

"Will you have to make changes to your women's program?"

He replied to the media with the comment: "The last I heard there were three periods to a hockey game. Come see me when the game is over."

At 3:19 in the third period, Hayley picked up a loose puck and bolted towards the net. This was it; she was going to score. She was going to tie up the game. When the puck landed in the back of the net, she rushed towards her teammates for a quick celebration.

Then the Jayna-Vicky-Lori line took to the ice.

The teams squared up at centre ice. The puck dropped. Vicky won the faceoff and sent the puck over to Jayna. Jayna dug in and skated towards the net, firing off a hard shot. Just six seconds had passed on the clock. Again the puck sailed to the back of the net. Now it was 4–3. Canada had the lead!

The Canadians scored three more goals in the third period to win the game 7–3. The goals were scored by the "old guard." Vicky popped one in on a pretty pass from Danielle. Cassie scored a beautiful unassisted goal. Thérèse slapped one in with less than a minute on the clock.

After the game, Danielle said to a *Calgary Sun* reporter, "The old guys got it done."

And when Cheryl was asked about the previous USA dominance over Canada and if the eight losses were still in her mind, she replied, "It has happened. It's over. It's done."

To that Vicky smiled and piped up, "They weren't handing out medals in

The Old Guard

Thirty-six year old Danielle Goyette was the oldest member of the 2002 Olympic Women's Hockey Team. But when she mentioned the "old guys" in her quote, she was also referring to the team's veteran players. Next oldest on the team was Thérèse Brisson, who was thirty-five years old at the Games. She had played in the 1998 Olympics and in five World Championships. Geraldine Heaney was the only player on the team to play in seven World Championships. In 1990, at the first IIHF Women's World Championships tournament, she scored a TSN highlight goal. She retired from the team after the 2002 Olympics, at the age of thirty-four.

those games. A great quality in our team is believing in each other and not getting uptight."

It wasn't just the "old guard" who talked to the reporters. Rookie player Tammy spoke with confidence to the *Winnipeg Free Press*. "We went after them. I don't think a freight train would have stopped us."

But the biggest comment came from Hayley. So far she was leading the team in scoring. She was considered a veteran at the young age of twenty-four. Articles were written about her; that she was the best women's hockey player in the world. She was direct and honest with the *Winnipeg Free Press* when she said, "One thing with our team this year, it seems that with everything that seems to happen, it happens with adversity."

9 The Battle Begins

The gold–medal game was played on Thursday, February 22, 2002.

Cassie, Hayley, Danielle, Geraldine, and Thérèse were in charge of the *quote du jour*. The five players got together. They wanted to do something different, so they got now–famous Olympic Canadian figure skating pair Jamie Salé and David Pelletier to talk to the team.

Jamie and David told the Canadian women to go after their dreams and not to give up, no matter what. Look what had happened to them, they said. They had skated a flawless performance, yet had been awarded the silver medal. They knew they had done their best. The North American media didn't like the results and one of the judges admitted she had not been honest. Jamie and David had been given the gold medal. Their emotional talk, about doing the best they could, inspired the Canadian women.

Although they had arranged for Jamie and David to speak to the team, Cassie, Hayley, Thérèse, Geraldine, and Danielle still had their *quote du jour*.

When addressing the team, all they said was: "*Carpe Diem*." This Latin expression means "Seize the Day!" or, in French, *Saisissez le Moment!*

That morning, Coach Danièle also left the players with some final words. "We will walk to the rink together, and when we are successful today, we will walk together forever. No one is allowed in our house today."

Coach Danièle talking to her team, keeping them focused.

When the Canadian women flew onto the ice, the stands were filled with plenty of Canadian fans wearing red and white, and lots of American fans wearing red, white, and blue.

The Canadian fans knew their team had recently lost eight in a row to the USA.

The American fans knew their team had a 35–0 record.

The warm-up for both teams was at a fast tempo. Earlier that morning, Kim had been told by Coach Danièle that she would be the starting goalie. After the tough semi-final game against the Finns, Danièle thought she was more prepared than the other goalies.

The puck dropped. Play began. And it was fast. Canada forechecked. Canada pressured. They played hard, aggressive hockey.

A thirty-second shift was all the players could handle. The game was too fast. They skated to the bench waving sticks. The next line was ready, eager to get on the ice and make this a game to remember.

One minute and forty-five seconds into the first period, Caroline, playing in her first Winter Olympics, saw a loose puck. First to the puck wins the battle, she knew. She raced to the puck. She pounced on it, picked it up, and fired it. When she saw it fly past the USA goalie, she screamed and jumped. Her teammates rushed over to her. Cherie picked up the assist. Two rookies had made that first goal happen.

Things looked good when the USA took a penalty at 6:17. But Canada didn't score on the power play. Then the USA took another penalty. Again for two minutes Canada tried to score. Canada's power play, once again, came out flat.

Then Jennifer took a tripping penalty. She skated to the box. The USA had a strong power play, but Canada had a strong

Kim St. Pierre getting in position to make a great glove save.

penalty kill. The penalty was almost over when Hayley took a delay-of-game penalty. The USA would have a five-on-three advantage for ten seconds.

The seconds ticked down. Canada killed one penalty. The gate opened, and Jennifer flew out of the box. The Canadians in the crowd cheered. Now the women just had to kill the rest of Hayley's penalty.

When Hayley finally returned to the game, the players pumped up the pressure. Five-on-five they were dominating the USA. They just had to stay out of the box.

Not even two minutes later, the referee put her arm up again. This time she pointed to Thérèse for bodychecking.

Players on the bench started talking about the penalties

"That wasn't a penalty."

"Why did she call that?"

Danielle, Jennifer, Dana, and Caroline hadn't played much in the past ten minutes. They weren't on the penalty-kill line. It was frustrating for them not to be able to play in such an important game, but they had to try to stay positive and keep team spirit up. They began to cheer loudly in support of their teammates.

When the referee put up her hand just

fifty-one seconds later, the Canadians groaned. Vicky got a two-minute penalty for cross-checking. The Canadians would again have to play for a minute with five-on-three.

Working hard, they killed both penalties.

When the buzzer sounded to end the period, the score was 1–0 for the Canadians.

They had played eight minutes out of twenty short-handed. To the crowd, the coaches, and the players, it seemed as if the American referee was making a lot of one-sided calls in favour of the home team.

The Canadians took to the ice in the second period determined to play five-on-five hockey. Five-on-five, they could win this game.

The puck dropped. The play started and went on for just over one minute. Then the referee put up her hand again. Becky was going to the box for hooking.

Yet again, the USA was going back on the power play.

Coach Danièle put out her first penalty-kill line. The USA moved the puck around in the Canadian zone. Back and forth. Finally, the defense rifled off a shot from the point. A USA player saw the puck and tipped it in. Kim didn't have a chance.

The USA had tied the game 1–1.

Back to five-on-five hockey, the Canadians refused to give up. Strong forechecking put the puck in the USA end. Danielle hadn't seen much ice in the first period. She wanted to do something. The loose puck was close. She picked it up and, on her backhand, sniped a shot at the USA goalie. Her shot was hard enough to send the rebound flying. On the blue line, Hayley saw the puck coming at her. Instead of waiting, she raced towards it. One stride, two strides . . . she was at the puck. With all her power, Hayley wound up and blasted a shot at the net. Hard and fast, the puck went high and straight upstairs, just under the crossbar.

At 2–1, the Canadians had reclaimed the lead.

Not even one minute later, the referee threw up her arm. She pointed to Caroline. Two minutes for roughing.

The Canadian crowd yelled that it was a cheap call. They were becoming extremely vocal about the number of penalties Canada was getting. Many were screaming at the referee.

Canada killed the penalty. Four minutes into the five-on-five the arm went up again. This time it was to Isabelle for tripping. With only a one-goal lead, Canada had to stay out of the box. But how, when the ref was calling everything?

Then Canada received yet another penalty less than a minute after Isabelle was out of the box, and the fans really screamed. As Jennifer skated to the box on a tripping call, Coach Danièle sent out her penalty-kill line.

Finally, the USA took a penalty. Canada went on the power play for over a minute. They cycled the puck; from wing to defense to wing to slot. The pressure was there, but the puck didn't make it past the USA goalie. When the USA penalty was

A New Olympic Sport

Women's hockey was introduced to the Winter Olympic Games in 1998 in Nagano, Japan. The United States won the gold medal, upsetting Canada 3-1. Players from the 2002 team who also played on the 1998 team were: Thérèse Brisson, Cassie Campbell, Geraldine Heaney, Becky Kellar, Jennifer Botterill, Lori Dupuis, Danielle Goyette, Janya Hefford, Vicky Sunohara, and Hayley Wickenheiser.

over, the game finally went back to five-on-five.

Canada felt more confident with the teams playing at even strength. Caroline rushed to the puck and battled. The USA player hammered at her. Then the referee blew her whistle. The USA would take a penalty and Canada would go on the power play.

But then the referee motioned for Caroline to go to the box, too. The USA had a roughing call and Canada, a holding call.

This was Canada's fifth penalty. They had played half the period short-handed.

The clock ticked down. Caroline and the USA player would have to sit in the box for the rest of the second period.

With only a few seconds left in the period, Jayna had the puck and saw an opening. She broke through and sent the puck past the USA goalie. She scored with just one second left on the clock!

When the buzzer sounded Canada went to the dressing room with a 3–1 lead.

10 Finishing Touches

The teams took to the ice for the third period. Not long in, the USA took a penalty. But then Canada took two back-to-back penalties. Becky got two minutes for roughing, and one minute after she was out of the box, Colleen got two minutes for bodychecking.

But the Canadians bore down and kept fighting. They iced the puck at every opportunity, forcing the USA players to skate to their own zone to pick it up. All the

Defense Cheryl Pounder works to tie a USA player up in front of the net so she can't score on Kim St. Pierre.

Canadians wanted to do was waste time.

If they could just keep their lead, they would win the gold.

With less then four minutes left in the game, the referee put her hand in the air. Canada touched the puck and the whistle blew. Kelly was going to the box for tripping.

The Canadian fans were irate. The American fans cheered.

The USA took possession of the puck off the faceoff. They set up in the Canadian end for their power play. The Canadian penalty-kill line hustled, trying to touch the puck. They needed to get it out and down the ice.

But the USA held on to the puck. They moved it around. The puck went back to a USA player at the point. A USA defense rifled a hard shot. It sailed past Kim and hit the back of the net.

The American fans went crazy.

With three minutes and thirty-three seconds left in the game, the USA was within one goal of catching Canada for a tie.

Everyone in the building knew that three minutes in hockey was a long time. There was still plenty of time for the USA to win the game. All it took was an unlucky bounce for the Canadians. The fans were on their feet. Fiery tension flamed through the arena. American fans yelled. Canadian fans yelled back.

On the bench, the Canadian players stayed calm. They still had the lead. They were still in the driver's seat.

Fans watched the clock. Players on the bench watched the clock.

The Canadians were so close. They just had to hold their lead.

Three minutes. Two minutes. The announcer made his "one minute left to play" call. The USA pulled their goalie. Six skaters against five. Canada had to hold on. They played with urgency, strength, and brains, but most of all, they played believing they could win this game.

When the final buzzer rang to end the gold-medal game in Salt Lake City, the Canadian Women's Hockey Team had won. They filled the arena with loud yells.

Forward Caroline Ouellette in front of the net putting the puck past the USA goalie.

Their arms were in the air. Gloves were tossed. Players mobbed one another.

The players skated around the rink, yelling and waving. Family members waved back, tears running down their faces. Canadian flags flew all over the arena.

The players draped the Canadian flag over their shoulders.

When the time came for the Canadian

flag to be raised, the Canadian Women's Hockey Team joined arm in arm. They rocked back and forth as they sang *O Canada* until their voices were hoarse.

11 What a Story!

The women stayed on the ice after the game, hugging and laughing and crying. Hayley brought her son on the ice and skated around holding him in her arms, kissing his forehead. With tear-stained faces and huge smiles, the players waved to their parents and friends in the crowd. They knew that family and friends had been there for them and had supported the team through their pre-Olympic struggle.

Instead of leaving the arena right after

With Canadian Flags draped around their shoulders, the Canadian Team and management staff line up to sing O Canada.

the game, the Canadian fans remained to watch the women. The game had been so dramatic. There had been so many penalties. Even the fans felt the emotional impact of the game and the tournament.

This team had overcome so much to win. They had had a rocky start, losing so many games. In Vancouver, after their eighth loss, when they could have given up, they had come together. They had cried then, too, but those weren't tears of joy. That had been their turning point. From that moment on, they believed that they could win and never wavered from their belief, despite what the critics said.

After the game, the media brought their cameras and microphones on to the ice. They wanted to talk to the players. This was a huge moment. Canada had broken their losing streak. After fifty years, hockey had come back and won an Olympic gold medal. The media slid

Kelly Béchard and Hayley Wickenheiser posing and having fun with their gold medals.

across the ice, hoping to get as many interviews as possible. The women were happy to talk.

When the *Toronto Star* approached Geraldine, she said, "Before the game, I was just thinking of how long I've played for the team; you know, winning seven world championships, a silver medal at the first Olympics...This is where I want it to end and to win a gold medal is perfect."

The players would miss Geraldine when she retired.

The captains of this team had worked so hard to keep the team together. The media lined up to speak with them. With her medal around her neck, Captain Cassie Campbell spoke to the *Toronto Star*. "Everything we've been through this year, it just seemed like what a story it's going to be, and I knew we were going to win."

Assistant Captain Hayley Wickenheiser also spoke to the *Toronto Star*. "It was very emotional. This team has been through a lot."

With a huge smile on her face, Vicky Sunohara told the *Toronto Sun*, "We had so much heart in our dressing room; we knew what we needed to do."

And they did know what they needed to do.

They needed to believe.

Epilogue

The women's stories spread in newspapers and magazines across Canada and in the USA. They were featured in *Maclean's*, *Time*, *The Hockey News*, and they even made *Sports Illustrated*.

The players became household names. This win raised interest in women's hockey. The sport now seemed to have more support from people all across Canada. Many were talking about how great women's hockey was to watch.

After coming home from Salt Lake City, rookie Kelly Béchard talked to her local paper, the *Saskatoon Leader Post*. "We faced a lot of adversity and had a lot of challenges that we had to overcome. We've had a lot of ups and downs over the last month. We've just gotten better and better every time we stepped on the ice. It got to the point where we didn't even question for a second if we could beat the Americans. I'm really excited to bring a gold medal back and see all my family and friends in Sedley and Regina. I know they've all been rooting for me and helping me all the way and it's going to be very special."

Another rookie, Colleen Sostorics, also told the *Saskatoon Leader Post*, "It's Canadian blood. We just know that when it counts we're going to come together and we're going to play as a team. It's kind of like you're pulling something from deep down inside you. It's one of the best feelings."

After the 2002 Olympics, registration across the country for women's hockey grew. Ontario saw the biggest jump. It went from 30,280 female hockey players in 2001–2002 to 34,710 in the season following the Salt Lake City Olympics. Another big jump was in Alberta. In 2001–2002, 5,137 girls were registered in the province to play hockey, and in 2002–2003 they saw that number increase to 6,882. In British Columbia, the numbers went from 4,741 in 2001–2002 to 5,321 the fall after the Olympic win. Most provinces recorded an increase in registration. Across the country, almost 7,000 more girls registered to play hockey in the fall after the 2002 Winter Olympics.

This rise in young girls playing hockey is good for the sport. It creates better players who know the game because they are starting younger. When they reach higher levels, they can play the fast tempo Olympic-style game. This gives Canadian coaches more players to choose from. It makes the National Team program have more depth.

The win the women had in 2002 also gave young girls many role models. Years ago female hockey players looked to the male players as role models. Now, young girls look to female hockey players.

When Cheryl Pounder heard that six million television viewers had watched the game she told the Canadian Press, "We have changed the face of women's hockey."

Hayley Wickenheiser now runs a tour of cross-Canada hockey clinics for female players. "We really are very serious about being role models for young girls," she says.

Cassie Campbell has gone on to become a broadcaster for Hockey Night in

Canada. She runs a ball hockey tournament in Calgary, Alberta, to raise money for Ronald McDonald House. The tournament is extremely well attended because of her fame from winning an Olympic gold medal. Many other players also run hockey camps that have become popular for young girls in the summer.

It has also become socially acceptable for girls to sign up for hockey. It used to be that parents didn't want their girls playing hockey because they didn't think girls should play such a rough sport. But now girls sign up because their parents have watched the Olympics and seen how great a sport it is for women.

Young girls playing hockey now have something to strive for. They can try to excel and become National Team players. "Now, young girls have the Olympics," said Hayley. "That's our Stanley Cup."

Glossary

Breakaway: A player in full control of the puck, and having no opposing player between them and the other team's goalie or net.

Cross-checking: Using the shaft of the stick between the two hands to check an opponent at any height.

Cycling the puck: Passing the puck from player to player in the other team's zone. Players do this to try and create a clear opening to score. Usually, they pass the puck quite quickly.

Even strength or five-on-five: When both teams have all five players plus their goalies on the ice at the same time.

Faceoff: The action of the referee dropping the puck between the sticks of two opposing players to start or resume play.

High sticking: Carrying the stick or any part of the stick above the normal height of the shoulder.

Holding: When a player uses her hands on an opponent or the opponent's equipment to stop the opponent's progress.

Hooking: Using the blade of the stick in a pulling or tugging motion to stop an opponent.

Minor penalty: For a minor penalty, a player is sent off the ice for two minutes of actual playing time.

One-timing: Passing the puck to a teammate who immediately shoots the puck without stopping it first.

Penalty kill: A team with a player in the penalty box has to try to play short-handed and not let the other team score on them. If they are successful then they are said to have "killed the penalty."

Penalty: The result of an infraction to the rules.

Point: When a team is trying to score and they are in their opponent's zone, the area near the blue line and the boards is called "the point." Usually, the defense players position themselves on the point.

Power play: When a team is playing with all their players on the ice against a team that is short one player due to a penalty. The team with more players has the advantage and they are "on the power play."

Slashing: Hitting an opponent with the stick while holding the stick with one or both hands.

Slot: The area on the ice which is directly ahead of the goaltender between the faceoff circles on each side. This can be referred to as the "scoring area" as well.

Stood-on-her-head: The term used when a goalie stops shot after shot from her opposition and doesn't let the puck go in the net.

Unanswered goal: Scoring more than one goal in a row without the other team scoring in between.

Acknowledgements

It takes a supportive crowd to write a Recordbook. I would like to thank André Brin, Aaron Wilson, and Jennifer Robins at Hockey Canada for providing me with photos and information on this team. I would also like to thank all the players who responded to my e-mails, the ones where I asked a ton of questions. I so appreciate your time and energy. Sami Jo Small put together the most amazing scrapbook of this team's journey to the Olympics and it was like a precious stone to me as it gave me insight into each player and to the tournament. Carrie Gleason, my editor at Lorimer, was patient and insightful with her edits. I thank her and the Lorimer team. And finally, I would like to thank my husband, Bob Nicholson, because without him I would not have attended the 2002 Winter Olympics, nor would I have been able to watch these amazing women win their gold medal. I was lucky to be there as a fan, and I knew that it was a great story worth telling.

About the Author

Lorna Schultz Nicholson is a full-time writer in Calgary, Alberta, where she lives with her husband, Hockey Canada President Bob Nicholson, and their three children. She is the author of a fiction hockey series in the Lorimer Sports Stories, including *Too Many Men* which was nominated for the Diamond Willow award. Lorna is the author of *Pink Power* and *Fighting for Gold* in the Recordbooks series.

Photo Credits

Thanks to Hockey Canada for providing all of the photos, including front and back cover, for this book.

Index

More gripping underdog tales of sheer determination and talent!

RECORDBOOKS

Recordbooks are action-packed true stories of Canadian athletes who have changed the face of sport. Check out these titles available at bookstores or your local library, or order them online at www.lorimer.ca.